The Creation Ser
A Bible-based Re

CW00348478

Plants and Lights

Carole Leah
and Sharon Rentta

NOTE TO PARENTS AND TEACHERS

The Creation Series consists of eight books based on the Genesis account in the Bible. This is the third book of this series and has been written from a Christian viewpoint. It is intended to be read *to* 3-4 year olds. The whole series prepares children to read and extend their vocabulary. In this book children can develop and practise preparatory skills for reading as well as be aware of God's power and his attention to detail.

BIBLE REFERENCES

All Bible references are in bold throughout and are as follows: p8: Genesis 1:12; p12: Genesis 1:18.

ENCOURAGE CHILDREN TO:

* Talk about the illustrations and retell the story in their own words.
* Look out for different shapes of the moon at night.
* Sort real fruits and vegetables into two piles and into colours.
* Learn the Bible verse and its reference (see page 24).
* Thank God for their favourite foods.
* Talk about the seasons (see pages 14-21).
* Ensure that children know the meaning of these words: *blossom* (flowers on bushes or trees); *enjoy* (like, love); *glory* (greatness, beauty, all lovely); *mist* (wet cloud near the earth); *share* (to give away); *thankful* (full of thanks).

Carole Leah became a Christian at a youth camp when she was seventeen years old while reading a Gideon New Testament. She felt called to write these books so that young children would learn the truth about God while also developing their reading and vocabulary skills. Several people have worked alongside Carole as she wrote this material but she would like to especially dedicate these books to the memory of her dear friend Ruth Martin who gave so much support.

Scripture quotations on pages 8 and 12 are from the Good News Translation in Today's English Version - Second Edition Copyright © 1992 by American Bible Society. Used by Permission.
Scripture quotation on page 24 is from the New Revised Standard Version Bible, copyright 1989, Division of Christian Education of the National Council of the Churches of Christ in the United States of America. Used by permission.
All rights reserved.
Text copyright © Carole Leah. Illustrations copyright © Sharon Rentta.
ISBN: 978-1-84550-531-8 Published by Christian Focus Publications, Geanies House, Fearn, Tain, Ross-shire, IV20 1TW, Scotland, U.K.
www.christianfocus.com

2

Todd, Joy and Daniel are outside their homes.
See what they are doing in this book!

Todd is outside his home.

Joy and Daniel are outside their home.

Look for the daisy flowers.

Can you find more than 10 pictures of daisies in this book?

Did you know that daisies close their petals at night and open them again in the day?

In the beginning

no plants grew on the Earth.

There were no lights in the heavens.

God spoke and

plants began to grow.

Mist came from the ground and

watered them.

God made pretty flowers of every colour.

God made juicy fruits and

crunchy vegetables of all kinds.

God made all the plants.

...God was pleased with what he saw.

Then, God spoke again and

lights began to shine above the sky.

He made two big lights.

The sun was made to shine in the day.

The moon was made to shine at night.

God made the stars.

...God was pleased with what he saw.

Now, Daniel and Joy can smell beautiful blossom.

They can climb strong trees.

Now, Todd can hear the corn moving in the wind.

He can feel the heat of the sun.

Joy and Daniel love to see the moon

lighting up the sky.

They like the different shapes of the moon.

Todd likes to watch the twinkling stars.

There are too many for him to count.

Todd, Joy and Daniel are happy.

They are thankful

because God gives them so much to enjoy.

God gives us plants to share and enjoy.

His sun, moon and

stars give us days, months and years.

The heavens are telling

the glory of God...

Psalm 19, verse 1